ESSENTIAL POETS SERIES 169

LAURA BOSS

FLASHLIGHT

*For Linda —
Dear Friend —
Gifted Poet —
Love,
Laura
11-23-10*

GUERNICA
TORONTO·BUFFALO·LANCASTER (U.K.)
2010

Copyright © 2010, Laura Boss and Guernica Editions Inc.
All rights reserved.
The use of any part of this publication, reproduced, transmitted in any form or by any means,
electronic, mechanical, photocopying, recording or otherwise stored in a retrieval system,
without the prior consent of the publisher is an infringement of the copyright law.

Antonio D'Alfonso, editor
Guernica Editions Inc.
P.O. Box 117, Station P, Toronto (ON), Canada M5S 2S6
2250 Military Road, Tonawanda, N.Y. 14150-6000 U.S.A.

Distributors:
University of Toronto Press Distribution,
5201 Dufferin Street, Toronto (ON), Canada M3H 5T8
Gazelle Book Services, White Cross Mills, High Town, Lancaster LA1 4XS U.K.

First edition.
Printed in Canada.

Legal Deposit – Fourth Quarter
Library of Congress Catalog Card Number: 2010925321
Library and Archives Canada Cataloguing in Publication
Boss, Laura, 1938-
Flashlight / Laura Boss.
(Essential poets series ; 169)
ISBN 978-1-55071-315-2
I. Title. II. Series: Essential poets series ; 169
PS3552.O763F53 2010   811'.54   C2010-905421-0

Contents

Airborne... 9
I Wanted to Go to Princeton 12
Of Course I Was a Virgin 15
My Refrigerator Talks to Me 17
Elizabeth Taylor and the Elastic Waisted Skirts 18
This Year 20
Queen Esther 21
When I Was Six 22
The Versailles Hotel 24
Last Row, Last Seat 26
The Only Man 28
Biology 29
Knitting 31
So It Goes 33
My Grandmother's Advice Was Simple 35
Baseball Memories 36
On Hearing of Gregory's Death 37
Net Worth 38
There Was a Time 40
I Still Need to Have a Boyfriend 41
The Enemy in My Apartment 43
Speaking to Aunt Lily Across the Years 44
After All the Other Babies... 46
At My Mother's 47
For Months 48
Watching Baby Bianca Take Her First Steps 51
In the Photo I Would Take if I Could 52
The Dodge Poetry Festival: Sunday 54
Lift Off 56
It's the First Night of Passover 58
Faculty Dinner: Montclair Adult School 59

If My Mother Could Speak to Me Now 61
At the Book Fair 63
After Abu Ghraib 64
Atlas 65
At the Reunion 67
Mountain Avenue: North Caldwell 68
Last Time 70
Burial 71
Astronomer 72
I Used to Be Thinner 73
At My Granddaughter... 75
My Son Is Running for President 77
In My Dreams 78

Acknowledgments 80

FLASHLIGHT

Airborne

*Listening to the Reports of JFK Jr.'s Plane Missing
After Leaving Caldwell Airport*

Years ago at Caldwell Airport,
    I left in a tiny plane
    my sixteen-year-old was piloting

The two of us in this one-engine seemingly
    "paper" plane he had pushed back with
    one hand while checking it before we left

I did not want to be in this plane,
    but it was just after I had separated
    from his father, and my guilt was
    making me try to please this son
    I had so displeased by leaving his father

The guy I was going with at the time
    had put his gold cross around my neck
    and was crying as we left – though
    his fear would not let him come up with us

My son said I was brave –
    All his friends who had come up with him
    were either screaming or throwing up at this
    point in the trip

We circled over New York City
    We headed up to Maine where
    my older son was going to school

There was no control tower person, but
    my son landed after a few more circles
Coming back from Maine that night
    my son told me to scan the horizon for planes
    too near to us

He told me I was right –
    He shouldn't be flying at night – that
    everything looked the same at night
He had me hold the map which he circled
    with his flashlight – trying to find out
    exactly where we were

I asked him if he had another battery for his
    flashlight – or even another flashlight –
    He said, "No"

I told him, I'd buy him another flashlight when we got back

He told me if for any reason he passes out
    or hits his head, I should click on a center
    radio station and they'd tell me how
    to fly the plane in

When we finally land, I ask him if his father has
    ever gone up with him
    "No," he replies. "He says he's not ready"
    (I'm not ready either I tell myself
    and I also think that my former husband
    is smarter than I thought he was)

But I also think how women try to please males –
    to so often do things they don't want to do
    just to please a man – whether it be family or a lover –

And I think how Carolyn Bessette
    who according to the news and family reports
    did not want JFK Jr. to fly his own plane
    and how she and even her older sister tried to please him –
    to show him that they did believe in him
    by climbing into that private plane

And I know how lucky I was when I got off that small
    one-engine plane at Caldwell Airport so many years ago

And I think how unlucky those other women were when
    leaving Caldwell Airport Friday night
    that good intentions, guilt, and, yes, and even love
    cannot always keep one airborne

I Wanted to Go to Princeton

I wanted to go to Princeton
    but I wasn't smart enough
And anyway they didn't take girls
    in those days
I wanted to go to Princeton
    but I didn't
And anyway it was my brother's
    job to go to a good school
    or at least get a scholarship
    to a decent school even
    if it were not Princeton
And it was my job if I couldn't go to
    Princeton to at least marry a guy
    who had gone to Princeton

So when I was at a female school
    Douglass twenty minutes from Princeton
    I dated Princeton guys not Rutgers
    guys whenever I could though I had
    to take a less attractive looking
    Princeton guy than I would have
    if I had been dating a Rutgers guy
    and the Princeton guy traded up in looks
    if he took out a Douglass girl rather
    than a Radcliffe or Vassar girl

And I could have married one guy from Princeton
    his name was Freddie and he was serious
    and thin and wrote me stacks of
    letters on stationery with a Princeton logo

and when his Princeton envelopes arrived,
I realized I liked the letters and stationery
more than I liked him

And another guy I dated from Princeton
nicknamed "Gish" was president of his
eating house, the only Jewish eating house
He would travel on the train sometimes to
see me at Douglass – And one weekend I
stayed over at that eating club while he as
president sat downstairs all night making
sure no guys got upstairs –
And I liked him but I liked him apparently
more than that blond Princeton guy liked me

And so my brother did what he was supposed to do –
earned his full scholarship to Rutgers, became a
Henry Rutgers Scholar along with his classmate
Robert Pinsky who was "good in English"
according to my brother –

And my brother went on to Yale Law School with a
scholarship like he was supposed to do –

And I married the son of one of the wealthiest Jewish men in
Passaic County – something I was supposed to do –
(though to my disappointment my husband had not
gone to Princeton or Harvard or even Yale but to
N.Y.U. Business School)

But he was smart and nice and nice looking and it was what
I was supposed to do –

After all I had gone to Douglass
    and after we were married
    had to transfer to where we lived in Rutherford to F.D.U. –
    And we all know no Princeton guy would
    have ever gone out with a girl from F.D.U.
    though William Carlos Williams lived in that little town in
    Rutherford – though I could finally concentrate
    on my courses now that I was married –
    (after all my job of getting married was now
     accomplished)

And my senses bloomed
    and my teacher brought my poems to William Carlos
    Williams
    and even my marks soared

And I loved that school and its English teachers
    as much and probably more
    than if I had been smart enough
    to get into Princeton

Of Course I Was a Virgin

Of course I was a virgin when I got married
    Technically of course
    It was expected in those years
    It was your personal dowry to your new husband

Of course I had done every possible kind of
    heavy petting without crossing that one step
    that would have made me "not a virgin"

Of course it was expected
Of course I wanted to with anyone I thought I might love
"Drive-ins" were not for the movies
The back of a car was not for other passengers
But still that virginity
That virginity was my Ph.D.
That virginity was my promise of a bank account
That virginity was my promise of a wedding ring
That virginity was me and every so-called "nice" girl –
    yes, I said girl – because that is what we were called
    and what we called ourselves
That virginity was my promise to him that his was the one
    penis I would ever feel inside me

Then one day I broke that promise
And walked away from that marriage door not unlike Nora
    in *The Dollhouse*
And now I try to remember the exact shape of his penis –
And I can't – well, not exactly
And I wonder if he remembers the shape of my vagina
I hear they're different shapes and sizes –
    no two exactly alike

Though we all know size doesn't count, it's technique
And now I can't remember the size and shape of each penis
Though some I remember
And I've slept with three Michael's
And three Bob's
And though I remember each man
I can't remember all their last or first names
And I don't remember each size, shape or shade of their penis
    Though I do remember one penis that was both half white
    and half brown
    (and while I was half crazy at the time of my divorce,
    it was at that moment that I realized the guy wasn't
    the person I thought he was since I had never seen
    a penis like that before)
But how clearly I remember each face
    (of a man I thought I loved)
And how clearly I remember each gesture of kindness –
I remember the most erotic men I've slept with –
And though they were not always the most technically adept
I realize that sometimes the ones I desired most were not
    necessarily the best in bed

And now one man for thirteen years
One penis inside me for thirteen years
    though obviously it wasn't in me for thirteen years
And I don't even care to study it
To distinguish it though it is so familiar to my body,
    to my mouth
Though I have found I love the man attached to it

My Refrigerator Talks to Me

Look at me
You've put all these family photos up
    covering my black steel door
You're on a diet
    (your usual start Monday morning –
    off Tuesday morning)
So I'm feeling empty and alone
    with only ice cubes
    in the freezer section
    and one solitary pint
    of cookie dough ice cream
    which I know you'll devour
    after the eleven o'clock news on Tuesday night
Inside me you have only a Diet Pepsi and some cream cheese
I am lonely
I miss your opening and closing my door every
    couple of hours when you're home to
    grab some left over pasta or orange juice –
    or cream cheese for your bagel
You pass me by and don't see the real me
Sometimes you smile at the family photos
    that cover the real me

Look at me
Put your hands on my door handle
Open me up –
Fill me with cantaloupes, avocados, half and half,
    meatloaf, and peach pie

Visit me often
Put your hands inside me again

Elizabeth Taylor and the Elastic Waisted Skirts

When I was growing up,
    I was told I looked like Elizabeth Taylor
This did not mean so much since my blonde
    attractive female friends were told they looked
    like Grace Kelly and my best friend Myrna who
    had short brown hair and what was called
    flat chested in those years was told she
    looked like Audrey Hepburn

I don't know about my other friends,
    but I would look up to this "older"
    (from my teenage view) movie star
    and be aware of how her life was
    going and if I not only "looked like her"
    but my life paralleled hers in some ways

So as the years went by, it seemed that
    she married someone wealthy
    then I married someone wealthy
And she got divorced, and I got divorced
    (though she was doing this with a
    volume fitting of movie star status)
She went with Richard Burton
    who drank and was charming and tempestuous
And I went with my version of Richard Burton
    who drank and was charming and tempestuous
    (though this was not evident to millions but
    only to a few of his friends and mine)
Then Elizabeth Taylor's waist expanded
    and my waist expanded

Then she lost weight
    and I lost my weight
She declared she would never wear skirts
    with elastic waists again
And I declared I would never wear skirts
    with elastic waists again
Then she gained all her weight back again
And I've gained all my weight back again
Now I'm not so flattered if people tell me I look
    like Elizabeth Taylor
Though I feel close to her as I look through
    my closet ignoring my tight-fitting zippered skirts
    while looking for an elastic waisted skirt that will fit
    knowing she is probably doing the same

This Year

My lover hasn't been out of his Manhattan apartment
    in more than thirteen months –
He's afraid the building manager wants to kill him
    for the landlord who has not had luck in evicting my love
    from his apartment his landlord can make a lot on

My son thinks the CIA is trying to kill him and barricades
    the doors each night so no one can get in

I walk my dog Coco along Boulevard East in a red and yellow
    wagon each day since her back legs don't work any more,
    pick her up out of the wagon near her favorite hydrant,
    put her back in the wagon and wheel her around for
    several blocks so she sees other dogs which she barks
    happily at so she has a bit of a social life as well as a bit
    of a breeze from this New Jersey side of the Hudson –
    Neighbors on Boulevard East walk by and wave
    and often ask me how I am –

"I'm worried about my dog," I say

Queen Esther

When I was five, my mother sent me to the Sholom Alechem
    after school –
We kids called it Yiddish school

I did not take to it and seemed to have great difficulty with
    any language but English –

The room was drab with each kid having a wooden seat
    with a desk attached to it –

I do remember that I liked my Yiddish name – Leba
My teacher told me it means love –
I remember that my Yiddish school teacher whose name
I don't remember asked me who in class would like to be
Queen Esther in the Purim Play – Every girl's hand shot up –

Then the teacher said whoever would be Queen Esther would
    have to have a gold costume –
Whose mother would make her a gold costume –

Only my hand went up – I guess even then I knew my mother
    would always do anything to help me even if it meant
    dyeing cotton cloth gold and staying up past midnight on
    work nights to sew a Queen Esther costume

When I Was Six

When I was six, my six year old friend Phyllis's mother died of cancer. We had all vaguely known she was sick but none of us children even thought in terms of her possibly dying. What I remember after being told of her death is sitting in the red clay dirt in front of my porch writing the date of her death over and over with a small fallen branch and crying to myself uncontrollably, while looking across the street at Phyllis playing and laughing and wondering why she wasn't crying, why she didn't seem to understand the enormity of what happened. Even then I somehow knew she would never see her mother again, that her world as she knew it would change radically.

My mother said I was too sensitive; I could tell she was upset about my reaction to this death. This calling me sensitive would follow me through my childhood years when I would get tears in my eyes if a teacher started to reprimand me unlike most of the other kids who would get belligerent. Nonplussed by my tearful reaction, the teachers would not yell at me but someone sitting next to me. I also tried not to get yelled at and never got anything but "A's" in deportment.

Eventually I learned not to cry except at moments of really extreme emotional pain and often not then either although I could feel myself crying inside myself.

Phyllis's Aunt Flo who had no kids of her own took Phyllis to live in New York City with her. Her brother Gary went to live in a different neighborhood in Perth Amboy with his Italian grandmother who wore the black of mourning for the rest of her life I was told. Phyllis's father a handsome milkman also moved into his mother's. Somehow we knew he was a heavy drinker, though how we children knew that I do not know. And so Phyllis's world was broken up by death and perhaps finances too. Somehow I was not surprised and for the rest of my life always understood how big an issue loss is whether it is through death or through love.

The Versailles Hotel

I don't recall if it were in Long Branch or West End –
I was only in fourth grade and even then showed
    signs of directional dyslexia that would haunt me
    throughout my life and annoy those with me
    when I was driving.
But I remember the Versailles Hotel
    with its ornate domed dining room,
    gold leaf on the ceiling.
At night the women in their "New Look" dresses,
    some of them actually real *Diors*,
    would tap their gold cigarette holders.
They smelled of Arpege unlike my mother
    who smelled of Apple Blossom
    some student had given her at Christmas.
The men smelled of Cuban cigars and money
    unlike my father who when his government job ended
    had taken this job as manager.

The Versailles Hotel with its private beach
    and path of petunias that led down to it –
    with the lifeguard Mr. Pierre (who wrestled professionally
    under that name) and one Tuesday when I went out too
    far and was too embarrassed to call for help, started out
    to help me.

And next to the Versailles Hotel was a crumbling Victorian
    mansion surrounded by honeysuckle – I would wander
    through its rooms wondering what happened to its family.
I thought it had something to do with money –
    or lack of money.

That summer I swore to myself when I was grown,
    I would give my parents this world of summer
    and glamour at the Versailles Hotel – My mother
    wearing that mink stole she wanted, my father with a
    Cuban cigar in his mouth playing cards with the
    men as a colleague not an employee –
Though who was to know that the hotel would burn down to
    the petunias, though who was to know that my father
    would die so young –

And while years later I did buy my mother that mink stole,
    I could not buy her anything that would take away
    the sadness she lived when my father died –
And I gave up my ten year old dream
    that I could actually buy happiness
    for those I love – and became a poet who still sometimes
    dreams of that summer at the Versailles Hotel.

Last Row, Last Seat

When I think of the odd child from school, I think of sixth grade and James Von Bront. I was almost twelve and sat in the last row, in the last seat, since my last name began with Z and Mrs. Skidlure always arranged the students in her class in alphabetical order. But this year she made a special concession for James Von Bront with his elegant sounding name among all the Ostrowskis, Kaufmans, and Romanos. I was still squinting nearsightedly at the blackboard from this last corner of the room and despite my glasses, I would see a 5 as a 3, and when adding would get an answer that although correct for the numbers I added was incorrect on Mrs. Skidlure's answer sheet and may have been a major reason of my shunning math for years in school and even today.

James was almost sixteen to everyone else's eleven or twelve except, of course for Mrs. Skidlure (in her hunter green suit and white crepe blouse or similar suit in another conservative color), whom we all knew was ancient (though probably only in her late sixties). Mrs. Skidlure, in her long-widowed state, who often mentioned she was a member of the *DAR* (something probably no one in that class would qualify for), lived next door to my favorite place – the Baron Library. Mrs. Skidlure who had her students collect dandelion leaves for her salad, who when asked if we could have the privilege of washing the boards tomorrow, would answer in a flat tone, "How do you know you're even going to be here tomorrow?"

Mrs. Skidlure, my first existentialist though I had not heard that word yet. But Mrs. Skidlure had a truly practical side as her having us kids collect dandelion greens for her salad proved. She placed James Von Bront as far from her as possible – right behind me in that last row in that last seat.

James Von Bront who never said one word in class that entire year of sixth grade – James Von Bront who was not only fifteen but rumors floated that he would drop out of school the day he turned sixteen and was allowed by law to do so – James Von Bront who at about 6'2" towered over my petite eleven-year-old height as well as even the taller twelve-year-old boys, James Von Bront who never spoke but would follow me every day after school as I walked home along the railroad tracks, six paces behind me as I walked home through the abandoned lots filled with weeds and, yes, some dandelions and scrub grass – six paces behind me for that long mile or mile and a half – But I remember feeling something was wrong, something was weird – James Von Bront never answered when anyone said "Hi" to him – never answered Mrs. Skidlure when she asked him anything – and after several weeks she never spoke to him again.

The only time he ever made any noise in class was once when he threw up behind me in class, and once in a while, if another sixth grade girl walked with me, he would, after she turned off near her house, still continue to follow me. So day after day James Von Bront would follow me home from sixth grade – I had the feeling if only I hadn't sat in front of him maybe he wouldn't have chosen me to follow home each day – and I became determined to get that *Z* out of my life, and when I was older determined to marry a man whose last name started with *A*, *B*, or *C* – I did marry a man whose last name started with *B*, but somehow I wondered if I would have married my ex-husband if a man whose name started with an *A* came along. Sometimes, like today, I wonder what happened to James Von Bront and if he had been trying to tell me something. Perhaps he was not a sixth grade stalker as I once thought, but a silent Lancelot wanting to protect me – to see me safely home.

The Only Man

The only man I could see my mother married to
    after my father died was Walter Cronkite
After all, he was practically family –
    in our living room each night
    reporting the news, his voice
    as familiar as my Uncle Ralph's,
    my mother's brother
Of course, Walter Cronkite was married
    which was a problem
But then my father had been married
    when he first met my mother
    though he didn't tell her
But somehow I trusted Walter Cronkite
    unlike my father
    to tell my mother he was married
And maybe like my father
    Walter Cronkite would love my mother enough to
    leave his wife –
    if he ever met my mother outside
    the TV in our tiny living room

Biology

Sometimes I wonder if I went into the arts
    as a way to avoid science
I remember Mr. Tompkins my biology teacher
    in high school who was also the assistant
    football coach
He was probably around twenty-eight –
    pretty ancient to a sixteen year old –
There were charts and drawings of plants
    and bones in that classroom –
His voice was boisterous as
    if we were his players and he was shouting directions
One day as I was trying to concentrate on
    his explanation of physical structure or
    bones or something –
He called my name and asked me to stand –
"Look at her," he boomed out to the class
"She is a perfect example of someone with a
    small bone structure"
"Turn around" he told me staring at me
    in a way that made me uncomfortable
    "Look at her bone structure" he said to
    the class, and I knew he was
And though I rarely if ever blush
    I could feel my face burning –
"OK, sit down," he told me
I waited to see if he would call on one of
    his football players in the class to
    stand up as an example of a large physique

He didn't. And though my teacher didn't touch me,
   didn't probably do anything against
   the rules, somehow I never forgot
   that moment in biology class –
   never took another science class
   if it weren't required

Knitting

Freshman year at Douglass the all female class
is knitting – None of the women near me take notes
though it is obvious the professor seriously stresses
certain key words in the Austen text –
He sees mufflers of all degrees of length growing
longer even as he lectures

Mufflers in Blue and White if the student has
a boyfriend at Columbia
Mufflers in Orange and Black if she has a boyfriend at
nearby Princeton though usually there is only one of those
mufflers since the Princeton guys don't usually take out
girls from Douglass but rather girls from
Radcliffe, Vassar, and even debutante Colby Junior College

But most of these expanding mufflers are Red and Black
for nearby Rutgers
And those girls who don't have boyfriends also
knit Red and Black scarves
These female students figure their best chance of getting
a guy is a Rutgers guy, and they are hopeful and knitting
These scarves grow longer and longer each class

I do not even try to knit
I am the only one not knitting
I am the girl who took the Singer Sewing Course
freshman year in high school and was thrown out
for not cutting on the bias, for forgetting to leave
room for seams

But there is something – though I can't
knit or sew or even fry eggs
but something in the way
this pen fits over my writer's bump that
grows poems

So It Goes

My mother did not want me
    to marry my husband
But I did
My mother wanted me
    to finish college
But I dropped out
My mother did not want me
    to leave my children
    and go back to college
But I did
I never really listened
    to my mother
She was smart enough
    to know that
But never stopped giving me
    her opinion

My grandmother did not want my mother
    to marry my father
But she did
My grandmother wanted my mother
    to marry the doctor she had been
    dating instead of my father who was
    struggling trying to make a living
    during the Depression
But my father put his hand on my mother's knee
    under the desk the first time he met her
    and was "fresh" my mother told me years later
My mother did not listen to her mother
But sometimes in retrospect, I think I should
    have listened to my mother more carefully

My mother always seemed perplexed that
   I didn't follow her advice –
Perhaps never realized she herself
   rarely followed the advice of
     her own mother

My Grandmother's Advice Was Simple

"No one can take away your education from you," my grandmother told me

That was easy enough to understand even though my grandmother had been going to night school for years trying to write English – even though she struggled with what we now call Dyslexia though she was smart enough to own a row of stores under her railroad apartment, smart enough to keep customers coming back for years to her grocery store where they came to her for advice and her sunny nature –

But her other advice to me – well, I wasn't so sure of

"What have you got to lose by giving away a kiss?" she'd tell me when I was fourteen and staying at her Brooklyn apartment for the summer

I didn't know much about symbolism at fourteen, but wondered, Did she mean only kiss – Was the kiss symbolic of more – much more – and what would my mother say if she heard this – my almost prudish mother who would ask me five years later what my fiancé and I could possibly talk about for so long on the brown velvet couch downstairs in the little stucco house in Woodbridge

Somehow I knew my mother wouldn't approve of my grandmother's advice –

Somehow my grandmother only gave me that advice when my mother was not around –

Baseball Memories

I have always been candid with the men in my life about
    not really liking baseball – not that I dislike it –
    It's just something that basically bores me

Still they seem to get pleasure in dragging me along with
    them to baseball games –
I remember when I was nineteen and
    my fiancé took me to a Yankee game –
    Actually, it was a double header; the highlight
    for me was the two hot dogs – one for each game –

And I remember the legendary Beat poet I lived with
    who took me to a game in San Francisco
    with his eight year old son – Why they
    couldn't go alone since he rarely saw him still puzzles me –

And I also remember the endless Little League games
    my own sons played, their father the coach –
    and how I pushed myself to go and cheer for
    them – though my younger son just stood forlornly
    out in right field for what seemed hours –

Yet I do remember when I was eight years old
    positive baseball memories driving home
    from my grandmother's with
    Mel Allen announcing the Yankee game on the radio
    and how soothingly his voice calling the
    game would lull me to sleep

On Hearing of Gregory's Death

Gregory, you once told me that we were
    going to spend our old age together
    I remember feeling petrified when
    you said that
Gregory, you once told me that if I were
    dying a painful death
    you'd come and give me something to kill me
    I remember I wasn't certain how to take that promise
But now with the news of your death
    flashing on the radio on Bloomberg News,
    I hope someone was there at that hospital
    in Minnesota where you had gone to live
    with your daughter who grew up abandoned
    as you grew up abandoned
Yes, I hope someone was there to give you
    that final shot and numb all pain forever

Net Worth

I don't know when I started losing control over my life. Perhaps it was after I lost all my money and got a statement from my stock brokerage firm that my net worth was thirteen cents. It was at that moment when I realized that the stamp on their envelope cost more than my net worth that I decided to look at money differently.

When I parked my car at a meter, I realized the quarter I put in was about 200% of my net worth. I started to look at my life in this new way. A can of fifty-nine cents dog food for Coco was more than four times my net worth, and she eats three cans a day. When I went to the supermarket with all the change I found in assorted jacket pockets from my closet and at the bottom of each of my rarely used pocketbooks, I thought I probably have less money on me than everyone in this store except the toddlers strapped in their mothers' shopping carts.

I do everything I can to get through this period. I stop at Whole Foods, the posh supermarket near me, when I'm hungry and eat sample orange slices they leave out. I eat their sample tortilla chips and accompanying salsa. Near the cookie section, I squirt myself with their tester body scents labeled *Brownie, Mowed Grass,* and my favorite *Waffles.* I don't buy anything. I think that the *Star-Ledger* whose front page I stop to read is slightly less than four times my net worth.

I go to the Salvation Army on Route 17 and look at clothes. All the yellow stickers are half-price. I look at a Jones blazer for $4.99 which means $2.50 today. I think about all the money I'm owed by my younger son whose mortgage money I gave him several years ago when my net worth was a lot higher than thirteen cents though he hasn't made a mortgage payment to me in three years though he would if he could. I think about the money I'm owed by a Trenton organization for a group of workshops I did three months ago. I think how my older son gave me an emergency credit card. I wonder if his new wife will grow to resent me as I use it for prescriptions and car repairs.

I think about how I once left so much money with a shrug just so glad to get out of the marriage. I think about how I never thought all those years ago that when I ran from money to freedom, how freedom also runs away when one has only thirty-six cents in her unraveling tapestry purse.

There Was a Time

There was a time when I was willing to do anything
for a man I loved
   leave my husband
   leave my children
   leave my money
And I did

Now so many years later I wonder how I could have been so
   crazy
   And I wonder if it were just raging hormones
But that seems too easy (after all I was in my late thirties)
Perhaps it was something stronger than sex –
   a deep need for love –
   for being in love –
that took precedence over
   money
   conscience
   common sense

But nearly twenty years later
   I know that I would never do that again
   for any man no matter how much I loved him
   no matter how much I desired him

Perhaps it's all the invisible emotional bruises
   from love that now protect me more than
   those once racing hormones that are now
   leisurely strolling through my system

and make me a more sensible woman –
and probably a much duller one

I Still Need to Have a Boyfriend

I still need to have a boyfriend
    even though I'm officially in AARP

Even if he hardly calls me
    except if he needs me to meet with his eviction
    lawyer at court

Even if we don't have the constant
    three-day sexual rendezvous
    that once ignited our lives

Even if he's willing to skip Valentine's Day
    or my birthday and just talk on the phone

Yes, I figure I'm embarrassingly at
    an emotional range level of a sixteen year old
    with this need to say, "I have a boyfriend" –
    not just to others
    but even more to myself

And it's true he doesn't go out
    with any other woman
Though how could he since he
    hasn't physically left his apartment
    in over two years (what with his fear of being evicted)

Though now he also has emphysema
    so how could we have the wild nights
    we once did since sometimes he gets
    so short of breath (though he is still smoking)

And what would it be like
    if we did make love
    on those rare times
    I go to see him
    and he strokes my back
    and talks to me
    and is the perceptive man
    I fell in love with twenty two years ago

Yes, what would it be like to make love
    as we used to – Would he suddenly
    gasp for breath thrusting in lust
    and climax with a heart attack –

Would I somehow with my bad back
    (I'm not in such perfect shape either, anymore)
    push him off me as he gasps not in lust but
    in possible dying – and dial 911 –

Would I need to give him artificial respiration
    (which I don't know)
    in the crotchless panties and
    thigh-high stockings he likes me to wear

And how would I greet the EMS workers –
    this senior citizen in thigh-high stockings
    holding a slipping sheet around her for modesty
    the peek-a-boo red satin bra partly showing

The Enemy in My Apartment

My enemy surrounds me
Boxes and boxes filled with
papers, poems, letters,
photos I have no time to go through
They invade my tiny apartment
They reproduce at midnight when I'm sleeping
I wake to more boxes of papers than I remember
from the night before
They silently remind me I need to open them up,
finish my manuscript,
or paste photos in an album
But the poems are the worst
They shout at me to work on them
I want to open my window –
open the boxes
throw these papers, these poems
into the Hudson River below
Let the fish eat these poems I'm drowning in

Speaking to Aunt Lily
Across the Years

Aunt Lily, if I could speak to you across the years
    (through all these years that you've been dead),
    I would tell you how sorry I am
Sorry for not visiting you the way my mother
    went to see you at Roosevelt Hospital
    every day after school – every day that you
    were in that hospital while they amputated
    one leg and then the other –
    that long year it took you to die
    while I was in my comfortable garden apartment
    in Rutherford still a fairly new bride, my belly
    starting to swell embarrassingly with the baby
    I would love more than I ever loved his father
And though I spoke to you every day on the phone, I
    never went to see you in that hospital that
    had once been only for TB patients –
    too afraid to risk my growing baby to germs –
    too afraid to say what he and I would get
    was in the hands of God or Kismet –
While you lingered through those dragged out
    long days, I sent you messages through my mother
Your own sister acting out her own emotional fear
    in not being able to see you more than once
    or twice in that setting –

Or was I too like your sister – not able to face
    your pain, entwine my fingers through yours
    and tell you comforting stories as you once
    told my brother and me at bedtime that year
    when I was four and you lived with us –

My son Barry was born in March –
    one month before you died on April 8th
In your will you left my brother and me
    everything you owned

After All the Other Babies Have Been Wheeled into Their Mothers' Rooms

After all the other babies have been wheeled into
    their mothers' rooms for the night
Amanda Rose, you are all alone in this hospital nursery,
    your mother in intensive care since you've been born –
    where she has only had chipped ice in twenty-four hours
    though tubes run through her arms
I stare at you through this glass wall meant
    for staring, adoring new grandparents
I stare at you; you seem to stare back though I know
    that this is impossible
I do not leave you alone
    though it is past visiting hours
    though this glass wall is a barrier to holding
    though the sky is turning murky
    over the nursery windows in back of you
    where the city's skyscrapers
    rise over Central Park beyond
    and the skyline seems
    both glittering
    and foreboding

At My Mother's

Right now at my mother's where I am staying tonight, as I did last night, my mother is probably trying to remember where I said I was going, though she asked four times in about six minutes as I was packing up my poetry books for the first workshop of the season. And she is probably wondering if I am coming back tonight though she asked me just before I left, and five minutes before that and a few minutes before that. And she is probably looking for my dog Coco (whose name she can't remember) after she sees its water dish on the kitchen floor and mini treats on one of her blue and white Corning plates for Coco so that's a hint I've been there – and the dog is somewhere in her apartment too

And she is probably walking around her apartment (without her cane though she is supposed to use a walker, which she never does) and checking under the Italian provincial fruitwood breakfront filled with delicate flowered porcelain cups and saucers she once collected – and checking under the bed where the dog goes when I'm there. And she is probably going to the refrigerator which has a list of my brother's and my phone numbers and tries to remember if she had dinner but takes nothing and sits at the dining room table and where she'll eat Hershey Kisses one after another – forgetting how many she's had though she's so thin now and this is all I know that really appeals to her now

And the television will be on – and she will be waiting for me to come back but wondering if I am coming back tonight – and she will go into the kitchen and wash the dishes again – and get more and more quiet inside herself and wonder if I am coming back

For Months

For months I have been wheeling my sweet dog Coco
(with her front paws that don't work) for her walks
I pick her up; place her in the red and blue plastic child
wagon
that I pull along Boulevard East – pick her up,
let her stand and wet –
Sometimes she hobbles a couple of steps –
most days not –
I wheel her several blocks, lifting her out,
placing her back in – at once was a
favorite hydrant or tree –
I stop by the neighbors walking their
dogs so the other dogs can sniff her –
She often sniffs back – seems content –
not in any pain –
Sometimes I take her by elevator to the dog run
at the bottom of my apartment complex –
I place her on the grass –
Sometimes she hobbles a few steps –
My neighbors with their dogs running
come over –
more sniffing –
She seems content –
At night I lift her into bed with me –
She seems content –
as she moves her rump with
a little thump next to my body
as she always has –
In the morning I take her down from the bed –
Sometimes she moves her body to an area
where she wets

I don't care anymore –
I clean it up with liquid soap and water
I don't yell at her for accidents anymore –
I place her near the dish of water and
Mighty Dog beef topped
with bits of American cheese –
She somehow slides herself over on
her two front legs and eats –
I feed her leftover *Boston Market* chicken,
her favorite
She seems content –
"She's not in pain," her long term vet tells me
But he can't figure out what's wrong with her
except a drop of arthritis which
isn't causing this – and she's a
little overweight –"Take her to the
orthopedist at Moradell Animal Hospital"
The orthopedist tells me it's not orthopedic –
but a skin problem –
"Take her to the dermatologist," he tells me
For six weeks I treat her skin problems
Her skin looks better
"It's orthopedic," the dermatologist tells
me once Coco's skin looks good
I take her back to the orthopedist
She seems content –
"I don't know what's wrong with her," he tells me
"If I were you, I'd put her to sleep"
"She seems content," I say
"She's not in pain"
I wheel my dog out of his office
in her newest plastic wagon –
(I go to an orthopedist myself
for my back which is getting worse

from pushing and placing my
thirty pound dog)
"I'll wheel her forever if I have to so long
as she's not in pain," I tell a dog owner
neighbor of mine
"She seems content," my neighbor says
"She's not in pain"
At midnight before Thanksgiving, I rush her
to Moradell Animal Hospital
We speed through the empty highway
usually filled with shoppers
or rush hour traffic
Coco is whining softly as I drive
The emergency vet is very gentle
For the first time both Coco's front and back legs
have not been working
My dog is whimpering – can't wet or poop –
My dog is in pain
She is not content –
"We can do exploratory surgery," this vet tells me;
"Your dog is not a good candidate for surgery –
She's ten years old, overweight, and the recuperation
will be painful and long and probably unsuccessful"
My dog is in pain
She is not content

When it is over, I get into my car
holding only her pink harness
with its brass medallion that says *Coco*

Watching Baby Bianca Take Her First Steps

After I leave my mother in her blue flowered hospital gown at Mountainside Hospital in Montclair, I rush to my daughter-in-law and son's house in North Caldwell to see the baby and where my dog Coco has been staying this past week since my mother's fall. "The baby took her first steps," her mother tells me and adds "Watch." Baby Bianca carefully lifts herself to a sitting position, then grabs the mahogany table and stands as her mother claps her hands as the baby gurgles and with effort wobbles forth moving from side to side looking like a rowboat in a sudden storm

This morning not so many miles away, my mother clutching a walker (the therapist holding her arm) takes her first step and starts to walk again

In the Photo I Would Take If I Could

In the photo I would take if I could, we are all gathered around my son Jeffrey's six week old infant daughter Bianca Elizabeth with her heart-shaped face like her mother's and her fringe of short lashes – Bianca Elizabeth (Elizabeth after the QE2 the ship she was *not* conceived on my son and daughter-in-law have told me – the ship that they both love to vacation on and have hung huge framed posters of all over the walls in their virtually furnitureless house). And it's odd to think that this nine pound baby is the namesake of a 68,000 ton ship, this tiny baby who struggles so with reflux (a disease I never heard of till now), a disease that keeps her from keeping her bottles down – (not so different in some strange way from the girl in the *Exorcist*) projecting forth a white gush of liquid, in this case the entire six ounces of milk she drank a half an hour ago, this tiny baby who continually makes gurgling noises to clear her throat though the $475 Manhattan specialist ("cash only, no checks or credit cards") says it is her immature digestive system and calls her problem "reflux" – Sweet baby Bianca Elizabeth, you are like a tiny ship – making chugging noises through each wave with great effort –

And in this imaginary photo I would take, my son Jeffery would have on his beaming expression and his arm would be protectively around his wife Valerie's shoulders unlike the tempestuous money arguing distance I often see, and their beautiful three-year-old Amanda Rose would be sitting on Valerie's father's lap – "Abuelo" as Amanda Rose calls him – instead this night as I am writing this poem he is in his hospital bed in Beth Israel with oxygen tubes and pneumonia from his chemo-weakened immune system – and with his daughter Valerie and my son Jeff making a decision this weekend to honor his month's earlier request that no extra life support systems ever be used on him if it should come to that – and Valerie and Jeff deciding not to hook him up to a ventilator that looks like the next step and Valerie saying to me this morning that her father from his morphine state managed to say to her, "What do you think about all of this?"

And in this photo Valerie's mother would be smiling without the worry that has climbed into her smile these past months, her hair freshly done and her nails newly manicured in deep plum which was the immaculate way she always appeared until six months ago when she had "no time for anyone but Vinnie" though she took Amanda Rose and sometimes infant Bianca Elizabeth on weekends.

And in this photo would be my mother with her sharp edge and inquisitive look that has disappeared this last year with her words "my memory is my problem" and asks me my brother's daughter's name – and in this family photo would be my older son Barry and his wife whom I see only four times a year because of distance, his seven day work schedule, and maybe something I put his wife off about though I'm not sure and in their arms would be their own baby they've wanted to have this past year.

And in this photo I wish I could take today would be my father – dead now these forty some years since my brother was thirteen and I was sixteen – and he would be smiling and not noticing how many years of this family photo he missed.

The Dodge Poetry Festival: Sunday

My coat is gone –
I somehow left it on the back of my chair
   in the Main Tent Saturday night

Oversatiated by hearing Lucille Clifton, Galway
   Kinnell, Coleman Barks –
   like a rich meal when suddenly you realize
   you overdid it –
I finally left before the Paul Winter Trio –
   after three days of giving poetry workshops
   though not reading as I once did in one of
   the smaller tents
I had faith that my coat would be there Sunday morning –

After all, my red flowered pocketbook that I had
   left hanging on the arm of the wooden
   chair in the food bungalow was still there
   when I ran back for it an hour later –
After all, these were poets –

But my coat was not where I had left it in the Main Tent
And it had not been turned in to Lost and Found
   or the Information Booth
Though I went back twice and the guy at the table was
   nice enough to take a fairly long walk to the trailer
   to see if it were locked in there –

After all, the coat did have a Donna Karan label –
After all, everyone thought my black trench coat was leather
   not plastic –
That's how good a plastic Donna Karan apparently uses

After all, it retailed at $554 which is expensive for plastic
> though I bought it for $54 at Loehmann's Clearance Center
So I figure maybe it wasn't a poet but a chair folder upper or
> a clean-up person who had a girlfriend he couldn't buy a
> Donna Karan coat for – and wanted to bring her a gift –

A gift of a really stylish, high fashion coat with epaulets –
> (and two lines of a new poem in the left pocket along with
> a crumpled tissue – probably all thrown out by now)

As this couple walk into church this Sunday morning, she
> strutting in what she thinks is a black leather Donna Karan
> trench coat, and he still happy and post-lovemaking
> mellow with this gift of love he gave her

Lift Off

Christmas Eve Day this year my daughter-in-law plucked my granddaughter Amanda Rose out of her suburban public school without a chance to say goodbye to the teacher Amanda Rose adored or even her best friend – and taxied Amanda Rose across the Hudson River to her other grandmother's to now live in a very neat apartment on a drug infested street known for its drive by shootings in Washington Heights

And my daughter-in-law has banned me from seeing my granddaughter whom I saw almost each day (first carpooling Amanda Rose and then helping my daughter-in-law who wasn't driving go food shopping and do necessary errands since she let her driver's license expire)

I think about how Amanda Rose when she was young and her mother was still working used to cling to me and call me "MaMa" and cry when I left after a dinner out or a trip to the town library –

And though I think I will be able to see my granddaughter once in awhile after my son signs the legal papers my daughter-in-law insists my son sign

When I think of Amanda Rose in one of the worst public schools in New York City where her mother and other grandmother register her as Puerto Rican and leave out the part about her being Jewish (since she was dunked in a tiny indoor Mikvah pool in a shul when she was six months old with my own mother in a flowered bathing suit and the official prayers that my daughter-in-law had agreed on with my son even before they were married)

And though I don't care especially about the "Jewish" part, I do care about Amanda Rose being in a school where teachers scream to keep discipline and her life has changed I know when I hear her eventually tell me on the phone, "Grandma, the boys in my class are so obnoxious" and "There's a girl in my class (who people said her father did something bad) who took off her shirt in front of all the boys"

Yes, and though I sometimes work as a poet with urban kids in Paterson, one of the teachers in Paterson tells me she knows the school my granddaughter is in and it makes this Paterson school look like the Exeter next to the school Amanda Rose is now in

And I feel helpless to help Amanda Rose as if she is in a space shuttle hurling through a lonely and dangerous universe with no connections to earth and I am the flight controller on earth helpless to communicate – to get her to safety

It's the First Night of Passover

It's the first night of Passover
    and I don't have much in my freezer
    except a dead dog
My son who has recently moved back with me
    since he has no place else
    to go though he is grown and the father of two young girls
    his wife took with her when she left Christmas Eve
    (a present to herself perhaps)
And my son believes in Cryogenics and has actually
    had his dog
    solidified in the necessary chemicals to do this
    "Woofie is only the second dog in the world to be frozen,"
    he tells me
    I say nothing

My son has decided to start a business freezing dead pets and
    also has me swear to freeze him if something happens
    to him though where the money would come from to do
    this is another thing

"I want to freeze you too," he tells me, "if you die
    from working too many hours"

But though I loved this dog that is now frozen –
    until they figure a way to bring Woofie back to life –
Somehow his presence in my freezer takes away my appetite
    not only for Passover dinner but also for any food –
    especially something cold

Faculty Dinner: Montclair Adult School

At the faculty dinner,
    my mother wears a
    name tag on her though she is not
    faculty
Though once again I bring her with
    me instead of a husband or
    lover
Though she as always is trim
    and neat in a ten-year-old tweed suit
But others are noticing her memory
    lapses and my mother who is
    not stupid realizes this
Someone asks her where she taught:
    I answer for her when I hear her
    hesitate ten seconds
Someone asks her how many years she taught
"Thirty-five years," she answers
"Good," I think to myself
Someone asks her what street in Montclair
    she lives on
She hesitates again
"Hawthorne Place," I answer to keep her
    from being embarrassed again
    though I think I'm coming off as pushy
But I don't care –
A woman who teaches acting on a different
    night offers to drive my mother the few blocks
    home so my mother and I don't have to leave early,
    so I'm not late getting back for my poetry writing class

      once I drop my mother off at her tiny
      garden apartment and rush back to this school
"What's her address?" the actress asks me, not my mother
"It's showing," I think though my mother
      and I use different ways to cover it up
But the acting teacher is patient and sweet
      through her fixed smile
      as she watches my mother search in a zippered tan
      purse from Hahne's (now closed for many years)
      for house keys
      to double check that my mother actually has them
"Did you lock your door?" I ask her quietly
"Yes, I think so," she says. "I always lock my door."
She finds her keys – holds them between her index finger
      and thumb – I rush to get her cane from under the table –
      kiss her goodbye – tell her I'll call her later

If My Mother Could Speak to Me Now

If my mother could speak to me now the way she did before
her memory erased so much, she'd say
    Why does your hair still look so messy?
Why are you still running all over for your son
    and granddaughters and getting
    only three hours of sleep?

Why are you still wasting your money on taking me out to a Chinese restaurant when I can't remember eating there five minutes later?

Why are you driving me to places I don't remember – even the Pathmark where I was once such a coupon collector? Bringing me to see my young great-granddaughters whose names I don't remember and whose faces I don't recognize though once as toddlers just several years ago those two girls loved to sleep in my bed with me and have me read to them *The Berenstain Bears* and Amanda would laugh at my hairnet I wore to sleep

And why are you spending your days getting sad – and yes, annoyed at me when I say I
    have to use the bathroom every five minutes

And why do you feel sad that I am now so quiet when once my tart criticism – though you know I was telling the truth – would make you so annoyed with me –

And why, why don't you know how deep my loss of not just memory but also independence is when you hear me say: "Where are we going?" and

"Let me hold on to you" when the world of the supermarket
seems a forest of caves and aisles I am lost in

And why don't you remember how independent I always was
teaching during the day, and an afterschool job at a private religious school teaching English, working two jobs and taking
college courses at night after your father died when you and
your brother were young teenagers and your father left no life
insurance
    and, yes, never leaning on a man for anything –
    Don't you know how hard it is for me to lean on you in
    this haze I live in
    where nothing stays in my memory for more
    than the moment it happens in –
    where your friend said, "Your mother has a glazed look –"

And try to remember who I was –
    nagging at you to look neater –

If I could remember, I'd take pills so that you would
    remember me the way I was
    rather than as this tiny woman with white hair
    (that she always remembered to dye) this fragile woman
clutching an empty
    pocketbook – and staring at you with glazed eyes – and
tightly grasping
    her daughter's hand

At the Book Fair

I am sitting at this book fair table (as I used to) and think this is where I met my last two lovers – Men come up and smile and introduce themselves – The fact that I edit a good poetry magazine is probably a plus, the way a big stock portfolio is to some individuals.

But, if I looked around then, I was often told that I was one of the prettiest poets at the fair though I knew not in the running with the best figure though I did my best in all black to hide this.

And it was at the book fair years ago that I met Gregory and he came back to get me at the end of the day – and soon after that we started living together. And it was a year later at the next Small Press Book Fair that my current long term lover came up to my magazine table and was what he calls "smitten" with me.

But now I am sixteen years older with definite smile lines and some light frown lines and not such a well defined chin line – and I gladly would trade in my present figure for my body I so criticized sixteen years ago –

And today while one man has definitely hit on me while I sit behind this table – my magazine flier with its list of poets like Allen Ginsberg, Ruth Stone, and Ishmael Reed does more for me than all the non-smear mascara I'm wearing.

After Abu Ghraib

After the horrors of Abu Ghraib prison
After the terrorism at the Russian school for children
 in Belsan
After the devastation last week from Hurricane Frances
After the ceremonies and memories yesterday on 9/11
Why do I stand so impatiently and, yes, annoyed
 as I wait fifteen minutes for an elevator

Atlas

My older son is the Atlas in our family
It's not fair to him, but that's what he's become

On Mother's Day my first visit since November to
    his house so many states away
    he fields his brother's frantic phone calls
    (with emergency problems)
    and spends 7/8 of his day
    unwinding these problems

And my older son gets an airline ticket for his brother
    to get home and gets him to promise he'll see
    his doctor in New York

I remember how earlier before the phone calls,
    my older son makes me early morning coffee
    won't let me clear the table (afraid perhaps
    of my messy ways)
I watch him load the dishwasher – take the baby
    from his wife and say "I'll change the diaper"
I watch him go to his computer in another room
    to work on a brief and prepare for court the next day
I see my son take on the role of Atlas
    in his own home though his wife is
    brainy and beautiful and more competent
    than I've ever been
    and a gourmet chef (which I've never been)
    stay-at-home mom
    to their baby and toddler son
I like the way my son tells me
    "Cathy is an amazing mother"

And this evening after my older son
    has solved (at least for today)
    my younger son's problems
    "I'm doing it so you don't have to"
    as he tries to hide his exhaustion
        and stress from the calls

Suddenly I see my son and his wife dancing
    in their tiled kitchen
    her swirling baby Marley
    him swirling baby Teddy
    singing as they whirl –
    smiling in this moment of dizzying delight –
    with incandescent light filling their kitchen
    where for this luminous moment
My son can drop his role as Atlas

At the Reunion

My name has been on my
high school reunion's list
of missing classmates
for more than four decades

But tonight (thanks to the
internet and an old friend's
research) I'm here
greeting a cheerleader
who is also a grandmother like me
"Do you know who I am?" she asks
recognizing me immediately
She has not put on her
name tag – "Tell me your first name"
I say thinking that might help and
she does – I say nothing and after several
seconds she tells me both her names –
And I recognize this woman once with long blonde hair
but now aluminum grey unlike the majority of the women
including me at this reunion who have colored their grey
in varying shades of ash blonde with a few of us
holding on to our old brunette but slightly lighter

And though I haven't thought of her for decades
I always liked her as I do now –
She's still thin (unlike me) but it's a different
thinness like a fragile older woman
as if she would not bend but snap apart
though the last time I saw her she was
leaping three feet off the ground twirling pompoms
and landing in a split when she was
the goddess of the football stadium.

Mountain Avenue: North Caldwell

Years ago, driving up the winding mountain road
away from all the bumper to bumper traffic I had just left
on Pompton Avenue and earlier on Route 46 West rush hour,
I suddenly had a sense of escaping not just from
the bad tempered drivers honking in frustration
(I wasn't so pure myself in that area)
And it wasn't just the lack of traffic,
as the road spiraled up between the walls of stone –
evergreens and crimson king maples and huge trees
set behind the cliffs, I circled higher and higher
as if even the air were fresher the higher I drove
as if I were climbing to a kind of fairyland
and all that was missing was the castle with
turrets and a prince waiting
(which probably was doubtful since
I was a twenty-one-year-old pregnant woman
with a husband and one year marriage)
That day I fell in love with a town
or maybe it was just a road –
a road that seemed to have the
power to wipe out all the stress of
the day just by driving up it –
just by its natural physical beauty –
I decided that I wanted to
live there – to drive up that spiraling road each
day to what seemed serenity from
day to day frustrations
My husband (whom I considered quite old
at twnty-two) and I had visited many towns in
Essex and Passaic Counties searching for
a place that could be permanent

(I still believed in the word permanent so
many years ago)
unlike our tiny garden apartment in Rutherford

And now decades later, I see a rerun
of *The Sopranos* which I never saw when it was on HBO
And tonight I watch
Tony Soprano leave the Lincoln Tunnel,
head south on the Turnpike, past the bridge near
what looks to me like the Pulaski Skyway,
past the oil refineries that don't pollute as they once did
unless you count visual pollution, past the ancient
brick walkup apartment houses and often neglected
treeless houses of struggling residents, past Cianci Street
in Paterson and Lou Costello's statue, past what looks like
Bellville's streets or Nutley's or Verona's
almost interchangeable at times
But when Tony Soprano starts up Mountain Avenue
in North Caldwell and he drives up that familiar curving road
   – as I once did,
I feel the same sense of leaving stress on some littered
   highway
   a mile below
rushing through me as I'm sure Tony does – even though
   it's TV,
even though it's imaginary – as perhaps in a way it always was

Last Time

for MB

Walking down the long hallway
of my now dead lover's apartment
as I have for twenty-three years
I realize this is the last time
I will probably ever be here again
I want to memorize all that I have lived
with for so many years but somehow
things blur like a Matisse tapestry of
patterns and layers
And I walk past the mug filled with yellow pencils
that have been resharpened and resharpened
past the empty box a VCR or an electric fan came in –
past the *Paris Review* posters
and the poster of Jane Fonda from her sex symbol stage
past the painted book case with glass doors
past the files filled with French translations
past the portable oxygen tank
And I smell the mixture of cigarette smoke, your sweat
on your ancient Harris tweed jacket hanging on a hook
I try to pack all the years I took for granted in my mind
knowing there's nothing more to do for you
knowing there's nothing more to say

Burial

for Michael Benedikt

Three people at your burial, my love of twenty-three years –
the administrative lawyer, a friend you hadn't
seen in more than a decade, and me
Here on a solitary hilltop in a new part of a cemetery
where your mother and father lie in the old section
Here where your old friend says Kaddish
though you with your Catholic father
and Jewish mother never went into a church
or synagogue in all the years I spent with you
Still, with the sound of the dirt falling
like sharp hail on your pine coffin
I break my promise to myself not to cry in front of others
Your old friend keeps chanting Kaddish through tears too
The state administrative lawyer that did not know you
looks uncomfortable but is kind and courteous and efficient
It has taken two months without my finding your will
before the authorities can legally allow you to be buried
I remember your telling me last year
with an almost concealed smile
that more than 400,000 had visited your poetry website

Astronomer

At thirteen, you traveled from one junior high to another
reading your paper on astronomy
that caused your teachers to want other students in the City to
hear your paper they considered
so brilliant from someone your age, or any age –
You tell me this after lovemaking years later, tell me
that giving that "lecture" gave you
even more pleasure than reading your poems
at the Library of Congress

Tonight, five months after your death that I am still recovering
from (and obviously you never will),
I look at the midnight sky and wonder, my love,
if your inquisitive spirit
is soaring past the planets like the mind astronaut
you always were

I Used to Be Thinner

I used to be thinner
I used to be prettier
I used to feel sparks of lust
I used to fall in love
I used to be less cynical

Now I might be wiser,
don't get on the back of a
motorcycle in Cancun
with a guy I met ten minutes ago
and ride to the beach to be
alone with him

And at poetry readings,
I don't have the featured poet
come up to me like years ago
and say, "I read to you tonight"

I still trust what people tell me
when I first hear it,
but maybe not
fifteen minutes later

I still have faith my son will
recover from his fears about
the government trying to kill him

I still dream of my
boyfriend of twenty-three years
and am happy for these visits
though I wake up
and realize he is still gone

I still cannot tell my son
to leave my house
and live on the street

At My Granddaughter Amanda Rose's 8th Grade Graduation from Mott Hall Public School for Gifted Students in Harlem

Before Bill Clinton gives the Keynote Speaker Address
telling these students and their parents and grandparents
   (and TV cameras as well)
that he like they had so few monetary things and
like so many of them no father,
that he like they had the brains, drive, and dreams and
says all these meant to be inspiring things which somehow are
judging by the attention of both the students
and the rest of the audience –
which is not so different from what Congressman
Charles Rangel said
as he introduced Bill Clinton and said how the Congressman
had been a kid himself from 133rd Street whose father had
been an elevator man in City Hall down-town –
And the audience is applauding
But I am still focused on Amanda Rose and how she earlier
gave the Salutatorian speech
and read it slowly and clearly and I heard it for the first time
I think how moments before that I burst into tears
as she led the two-by-two procession of the eighth-grade class
of hundreds into the auditorium side by side
with the Valedictorian ("a tenth of a tenth of a point
between them" my granddaughter told me) –
both the only two
wearing gold sashes over their graduation robes – both with
smiles that seemed to stretch beyond this moment,

beyond all the work that has brought them to this moment
beyond the gold medals for Presidential Education Award
the two will share on stage, beyond the medals my grand-
daughter will get for English and for Service –
beyond all the brightness in this room of all
these gifted students, so that the 42nd President (who has his
office in their neighborhood, he tells them) and says nothing
is more important to America than what these students
    will contribute –
And the audience cheers and for a moment
we all believe as Clinton says that America is
    the greatest place to live
and the future because of these kids who will contribute
    by helping others –
will be good and safe and shining

My Son Is Running for President

Every mother dreams of her son running for President
And mine is

He's on the ballot in my state though not others
(because of lack of campaign funds)
He has worked twelve hour days for a year
to get his name on the ballot as an independent
He has wandered through the unknown forests
of government regulations and filing complexities

He calls his independent party the Vote Here
Party hoping some people who aren't in the top
IQ tiers of voters will think they have to Vote Here
He has always had a good sense of humor
He has always been bright
He has always been my Dennis the Menace kid
And though I know it would be the American Dream
come true for most mothers
And though I am proud my son has been able to achieve
his American Dream
And though for a moment when I enter the voting booth
and just in that isolated moment feel a dizzying thrill
to see his name listed next to Obama and McCain
And though I normally would press the lever for Obama,
I press the lever for President for my son
Though I know he has no real chance of winning
Though when I walk out of the booth,
Still I once again realize I would rather have him
working at a regular job

In My Dream

In my dream, Michael, my boyfriend of twenty-three years
    returns from the dead though he's only been
    dead these two long months (and only actually
    buried since Friday)
And I remind him that I cannot find his will
    and what he didn't want to happen – all his poems,
    and his bank accounts, all his archives, all his property
    will go to the cousin he hated and hadn't
    seen in sixteen years instead of going to me,
    his supposed beloved who was with him when
    he died here in his Manhattan apartment
And I am so happy to see him back in his apartment
    and I am somehow here too though I had to leave
    several days after he died since I wasn't on the
    lease and when I called the cousin because I had
    no authority to bury Michael legally and thought it
    practical that he be buried or cremated rather
    than just lying in some funeral home where they
    told me very politely, if not subtly menacingly, they
    were going to give his body to the city which would
    dump him in a pauper's grave though my love
    was not a pauper by any means
And the cousin, when I called him, told me to send him
    the keys which my love had given me as well
    as Michael's own keys since I had no legal
    right to be in the apartment
And the cousin was polite after his initial diatribe about
    Michael's "horrible treatment" of Michael's mother

But now Michael is back and so happy to see me,
    but I'm so stressed out about the will and urge him
    to go with me to the bank to make out a new will
    before he has to return to the dead
And I briefly wonder how it will seem to Michael's cousin
    to have a will made out after Michael's death
    but with it notarized and his genuine signature
    and both witnesses

And we have to wait a long time where
    you sit at the bank when the officers are busy
    and I am so stressed that it won't get done
    before Michael dies again and goes back
    to the dead
And I feel the way, only more so – the way I felt this dread,
    my stomach anxiety before my math part of the GRE –
At the same time I am making Michael feel stressed
    but he wants to get his will done so his stuff –
    all the money, all his poems – go to me
    since he knows this cousin he hates
    has no interest in Michael or Michael's work
    just the money

And Michael insists as he always did on reading the papers
    very carefully as he always read his legal stuff –

And finally takes out his pen to sign
    just as I wake up with a prism of morning light
    through my bedroom window reflecting
    the Hudson River below
    and the skyline above it
    and where I can see in the far distance
    the corner of Michael's apartment house across the river

Acknowledgments

Acknowledgment is due, with thanks, to the editors and publishers of the following periodicals and anthologies where some of these poems first appeared: *The American Voice in Poetry: The Legacy of Whitman, Williams, and Ginsberg* (Poetry Center, PCCC 2010), *The Carriage House Poetry Series Tenth Anniversary Issue* (Muse Pie Press, 2009), *Connecticut Review, Edison Literary Review, Idiom, Jewish Women's Literary Anthology, The Journal of New Jersey Poets, The Literary Review, Lips* ("Michael Benedikt Memorial Issue"), *Long Shot, Microcosm, Mobius, The New York Quarterly, The Paterson Literary Review, Poetic Reflections* (Northwind, 2004), *The Poetry of Place: North Jersey in Poetry* (Poetry Center, PCCC, 2008), *The Poets of New Jersey* (Jersey Shore Publications, 2005), *Searching for Daylight* (Gatehouse, 2002), *Seventh Quarry* (Wales), *Solo Café, Tiferet, Red Wheelbarrow.* I am grateful to the New Jersey State Council on the Arts/Department of State for Creative Writing Fellowships in Poetry (1986, 1992 and 1999) which gave me the time to work on this manuscript.

Laura Boss, a national award-winning poet, is a first prize winner in Poetry Society of America's Gordon Barber Poetry Contest and in 1998 was one of ten finalists in the country in PSA's Alice Fay Castagnola contest for a manuscript. Founder and editor of *Lips* poetry magazine, she was the sole representative of the USA in 1987 at the XXVI Annual International Struga Poetry Readings in Europe. In 2007, she read abroad at the Dylan Thomas Centre in Wales. Her awards for her own poetry also include an American Literary Translators Award (funded through the National Endowment for the Arts) for her book *On the Edge of the Hudson* to be translated into a bilingual (English-Italian) edition; and Fellowships in Creative Writing (Poetry) from the New Jersey State Council on the Arts/Department of State in 1999, 1992, and 1986. A Geraldine R. Dodge Poet, she has been a featured reader as a Festival Poet at the 2010 Geraldine R. Dodgne Poetry Festival at NJPAC. Her books of poetry include *Stripping* (Chantry Press, 1982), the ALTA award-winning *On the Edge of the Hudson* (Cross-Cultural Communications, 1986), *Reports from the Front* (Cross-Cultural Communications, 1995), which was nominated for an American Book Award, and *Arms: New and Selected Poems* (Guernica Editions, 1999). Her poetry has appeared in *The New York Times*.

Marquis Book Printing inc.
Québec, Canada
2010